LOOK THE PART

THE WORKBOOK

LAURA MARIANI

ALSO BY LAURA MARIANI

Fiction

Gabrielle, from the diary of (The Nine Lives of Gabrielle #1)

A vivid portrait of one day in a woman's life through her morning pages.

The city of London during lockdown the background.

Non-Fiction

STOP IT! It is all in your head

The RULE BOOK to Smash The infamous glass ceiling - For women & young women everywhere — personal transformation & success 101.

The Think, Look & Act The Part Series.

Think The Part

Upgrade your consciousness and mind-set. Make winning a key part

Act The Part

A personal coach to act in spite of fear, right here, right now.

More non-fiction books and courses are coming soon. Keep an eye for new releases, giveaways and pre-release specials by checking at www.thepeopleal-chemist.com

You can also buy books and courses directly from the author at www.payhip.com/LauraMariani

ABOUT THE AUTHOR

Laura Mariani is an Author, Speaker and Entrepreneur.

She started her consulting business after a successful career as Senior HR Director within global brands in FMCG, Retail, Media and Pharma.

Laura is incredibly passionate about helping other women to break through barriers limiting their personal and/or professional fulfillment. Her best selling nonfiction *STOP IT! It is all in your head* and the *THINK, LOOK & ACT THE PART* series have been described as success and transformation 101.

She is a Fellow of the Chartered Institute of Personnel & Development (FCIPD), Fellow of the Australian Human Resources Institute (FAHRI), Fellow of the Institute of Leadership & Management (FInstLM), Member of the Society of Human Resources Management (SHRM) and Member of the Change Institute.

She is based in London, England with a strong penchant for travel and visiting new places. She is a food lover, ballet fanatic, passionate about music, art, theatre. She likes painting and drawing (for self-expression not selling but hey, you never know...), tennis, rugby, and of course fashion (the Pope is Catholic after all).

www.thepeoplealchemist.com

twitter.com/PeopleAlchemist
instagram.com/lauramariani_author
linkedin.com/in/lauramariani-fcipd

CONTENTS

INTRODUCTION

Women on Boards, or lack of them, is still a current topic — if you are looking at top global companies worldwide women in leadership represent 12% of the total (depending on what research is taken into consideration and the number of companies surveyed).

International Women's Day has a pledge every year, and each year we go around the same merry-go-round, new legislation, new pledges, new campaigns and there we go again.

According to recent research carried out at the BI Norwegian Business School by Professor Øyvind L. Martinsen and Professor Lars Glasø, women are better suited at leadership than men based on five personality traits, which can be measured for effective leadership. The study surveyed more than 2,900 managers to ascertain leadership personality traits.

Women scored higher in:

- Initiative and clear communication;
- Openness and ability to innovate;

- Sociability and supportiveness; and
- Methodical management and goal setting.

So, if women possess most of the qualities necessary to be a leader, what is stopping them? Lack of visible female leadership and role models has certainly played a part, same as cultural and family paradigms, sexism, racism, ageism and all other isms out there.

Human beings throughout history, however (including women) have overcome obstacles that seemed insurmountable to achieve their dreams/justice or whatever it is they wanted during times when overcoming these obstacles represented everything that was not "the right thing to do", during times when laws were against them.

Did this stop them? Of course not, they fought and found a way, because the what and why were bigger than the "No you can't".

There were people who accepted the way things were and conformed, still are, people that think that things are unfair, the state should do more, religion should do more, someone else should do more, always someone else.

You know what? It is time to STOP IT!!! Stop giving power to external forces and let them control your life.

STOP IT!

Smash that ceiling, and I mean the ceiling in your head, the only thing that is truly stopping you to achieve what you really want, and if that is being CEO of some company or Prime Minister/President or whatever, so be it.

My goal is for you to realize that, once you have truly come to terms with what you really want for your life and why you really want it, once you have controlled your mind and believe, you will be unstoppable.

I hope this workbook becomes one of the many steps taking you where you want to go.

Stop it! It is all in your head – Smash Your Ceiling.

Laura xxx

Why this workbook

I wrote my book "STOP IT! It is all in your head" as a call to action for women like you to take ownership and responsibility for their career and climb that ladder all the way up to the ceiling and smash it, if that is what they wish.

In my career as a corporate human resource director I had seen too many talented women selling themselves short and missing out on opportunities, not because there were none (there were and ready for the taking) but because of the way they approached the whole thing.
I wanted to help and break down the biggest barrier of all:

- Mindset.

I wrote the book as a practical, no-nonsense guide, with some exercises to start the process along and move people in the right direction.

This workbook, together with the other two workbooks, "Think The Part " and "Act The Part", is the next step forward, transforming and enlarging your perceptions, and challenging and overthrowing some of your negative beliefs about yourself and your environment.

"Look The Part" (and "Think The Part" or "Act The Part") is experiential and motivational rather than informational.

What does that mean?

Very simply, it means that it works not by transferring a body of data from me to you. Its main function is to create an experience, which will in itself and of itself change the way you see yourself.

As always, what you will get out of it depends largely on what you contribute to it and your commitment to follow through.

The workbook is also designed to affect the whole person and free up your capacity for self-expression, drawing upon not just the thinking analytical mind but also imagination and intuition.

It helps you to discover how your own personal belief system stands in your own way of success and then take you there, after you have truly decided where that is and why you really want it.

If you are frustrated, annoyed, disillusioned, you are going to project that into your professional and personal life.

Time to adopt airlines' guidelines — put your oxygen mask first and start flying free!

PREFACE

How to use this workbook

This workbook is part of a series of three (Think, Look and Act The Part) and was written both as an accompaniment and complement to the "STOP IT! It is all in your head" book but also a stand-alone self-discovery self-empowerment workbook and can be used in these different ways:

1. In combination with the STOP IT! Book and the other two workbooks ("Think The Part" and "Act The Part")
2. In combination with the book
3. As a stand alone workbook

Option 1 - STOP IT! Book + the three workbooks

You have decided to go all in and immerse yourself in this journey, congratulations!!

I recommend that you start by firstly reading the book in full (skip the exercises) and then start with the workbooks in sequential order e.g.

"Think The Part" first, then "Look The Part" and finally "Act The Part" (it all starts with the mind you see …).

The workbooks are following the order/chapter sequence of the book with far more exercises of course (otherwise what's the point of the workbooks, right?), broken down into 30 consecutive days - 30 days to a more powerful self-image and belief system.

Don't be tempted to skip through it and do more than one day at the time.
     Instead of going fast, go deep into your feelings/fears and be honest with yourself.

And if you action one workbook at the time, and one straight after the other, you will go even deeper whilst also establishing some daily habits which hopefully you'll keep on-going.

When you go through the workbooks one at the time, some parts are the same: don't succumb to the temptation to skip the exercises.

Repeat them.

You will see that the second time around, you'll have different insights. Each time will give a deeper realization of yourself and release a higher and more powerful self-image. And if you use them in the context/theme of the workbook (Think, Look or Act) you will get even more benefits.

Option 2 - STOP IT! + This workbook

If you decided to go with the "STOP IT" book and this workbook, again congratulations!
     Again I recommend you start with reading the book in full, skipping the exercises and then proceed through the workbook one day at the time for the 30 days.

Option 3 - workbook alone

If you decided to go with just the workbook, still huge congratulations, a journey begins with the first step.

How to go through the workbook itself

The workbook is laid out as a journey for 30 consecutive days.

Each day begins with a Monkey Mind/"dump the c*** off your brain into a page" exercise.

Say what?????? You read it right: The Monkey Mind Exercise.

Put it simply, this is outpouring streams of consciousness on a page (or more) to start the day with a clear mind. It is a means to an end with neither right nor wrong way of doing it.

I first heard of this exercise via Tim Ferriss in "Tools of Titans". He was inspired by Julia Cameron in her "The Artist Way: Morning Pages Journal".

Write a minimum of a page (you'll see, some days you won't be able to stop at that). I will just supply you with an opening sentence/word; a prompt and then you'll write anything and everything that comes to mind.

If you don't feel like doing it, force yourself: it is like therapy but free.

Each day ends with 3 things you are grateful for/appreciate related to the topic discussed for that day — it doesn't matter how small and apparently insignificant.

Instead of talking about the usual suspects though (*grateful for health, children, the dog , etc., etc.*) use this as an opportunity to review things in the context of the day's subject.

If you can't find anything to be grateful for/appreciate for that given subject, think again — you are not looking hard enough.

By looking for things to appreciate, you are firstly training your mind to look for positive aspects. Secondly, and most importantly, you begin to recognize how many more opportunities you/we, as women, have now compared to the past, many of which we take for granted.

When to start

You should really start on a Sunday (Day 1) with the "Fear" exercise to unroot your fears from the unconscious mind and bring them to the surface.

Owning and acknowledging fears is a very powerful first step to disempowering them. It is the fears that we ignore and that have power over us.

And then from Day 2 onwards, Mondays to Fridays, is reading and exercises — daily (we are talking about 20 minutes or 30 if you'll have a cup of tea whilst doing them).

This avoids the IDIOS fallacy. That is an acronym for *I'll do it on Saturday,* and it is a fallacy because a) you won't, and b) if you do, you'll hate it for eating up time in your weekend.

On weekends you are kind of free; I'm saying kind of because you should still do the Monkey Mind brain dump in the morning and the 3 things to be grateful for in the evening.

If you wish to re-read and go over the week, by all means do, but don't force yourself. Spend time resting, recharging your batteries, doing the things you love with the people you love (or your errands if you have to…).

Time to start.

DAY 1: THERE IS NOTHING TO FEAR BUT FEAR ITSELF

The Monkey Mind/dump the c*** exercise

Prompt:

What comes to mind when thinking of the word fear?

....
....
....
....
....
....
....
....
....
....
....
....
....
....
....
....

The fear process

The fear process is one of the most powerful I have ever encountered; I discovered it when reading "Write For Your Life - The Home Seminar For Writers" by Lawrence Block.

I did it at that time and I have re-done it each time I start a new project/venture, both in my professional and personal life.

Fear contributes to our self-sabotage; it keeps us from extending ourselves and taking chances. So we need to bring it (or them) to the open and face it.

"Fear is the mind killer" - Frank Herbert.

Ready?

Ok, ready or not here it is — trust me; it is necessary to go through this.

I'm now going to quote literally from Lawrence Block's

"Write For Your Life" as the process is perfect as it is. It goes like this:

A fear I have about .... is that ....

1. If you run out of fears, make something up — even if you're sure it's pure fabrication.
2. Don't attempt to judge the reality of your fears. If something comes to mind, don't try to figure out if it really and truly applies to you. Write it down anyway.
3. If a thought comes to mind and it's so disturbing that you don't want to permit yourself to write it down, write it down!
4. Don't censor your thoughts. And don't waste time telling yourself it doesn't make sense; it's not how you really feel. And don't get trapped by the notion that writing down the

thought will make it real. The object of this process is to let go of your fears, and you let go of them by releasing them from your mind and putting them down on the page.

Write as quickly as possible, following the process. Do not stop before you've written down at least a full page (thanks again to Lawrence Block for this process).

Before you start, think about what brought you here, your professional situation and what you are trying to achieve.

BREATHE.

Breathe again.

Turn the page and start the process.

Go ahead.

A fear I have about .... is that

Take a moment to write down some things that fear has kept you from doing throughout your life — things that you really wanted to do.

....
....
....
....
....
....
....
....
....
....
....
....
....
....
....
....
....
....
....
....
....
....
....
....
....
....
....
....
....

Done?

And now, to move on from here write the following:

"I am now willing to act in the presence of fear. I hereby resolve that I will never again allow fear to keep me from doing something I genuinely desire to do".

Then sign your name and date it.

....
....
....
....
....
....
....

Name ....

Date ....

Enough for today — good job!

3 things to be thankful for

Think back at the topic covered today — what are the 3 things you are grateful for, despite everything? Remember, if you can't think of any — you are not looking hard enough. Think again.

....
....
....
....
....
....
....
....
....
....
....
....
....
....
....
....
....
....
....
....
....
....
....
....
....

You see? It wasn't that difficult, was it? Great work.

DAY 2: WHERE ARE YOU NOW?

The Monkey Mind/dump the c*** exercise

Prompt:

What comes to mind when thinking of diversity?

....
....
....
....
....
....
....
....
....
....
....
....
....
....

The Overview

We cannot deny that boardroom diversity is increasing although women remain underrepresented. Looking at recent research from Credit Suisse more than 3,000 global companies found that women held 14.7% of board seats in 2015, up by 54% from 2010 (The CS Gender 3000: The Reward for Change, - 2016).

In the Morgan Stanley Capital International (MSCI) study, Women on Boards: Global Trends in Gender Diversity on Corporate Boards, November 2015, out of the 4,218 companies covered women held 15% of board seats up from 12.4% the previous year (73.5% had at least one woman director and 20.1% had boards with at least three women) while in the Deloitte's analysis of nearly 6,000 companies in 49 countries (Women in the Boardroom: A Global Perspective) women held 12% of board seats, of which only 4% at board chair position.

Research from many worldwide organizations have found that three women or more are needed to create a "critical mass", which can lead to better financial performance yet only 20.1% have at least three women.

MSCI found that having three or more women changes the boardroom dynamics and "enhances the likelihood that women's voices and ideas are heard", also resulting in better financial results than those companies who had fewer like 16% higher Return on Sales (ROS), 26% higher Return on Invested Capital (ROIC) and higher Return on Equity (ROE) than companies without (10.1% vs. 7.4%), as well as a superior price-to-book ratio (1.76 vs. 1.56).

They also found incidentally that companies with fewer women on boards had more governance-related controversies than average.

The highest percentages of women on boards can be found in the old continent with Norway (46.7%), France (34.0%), and Sweden (33.6%) leading the way and the lowest in Taiwan (4.5%), South Korea (4.1%), and Japan (3.5%) — source Credit Suisse.

Countries with specific targets, quotas, and penalties for not meeting regulations have nearly doubled the average percentage of women on boards including the aforementioned Norway, Iceland, Finland, and Sweden
(+ 34%) compared to countries without those measures (+18%).

Action Point
It is time to do some research and raise your awareness on this subject, starting from looking at the sector where you are currently working in, or the one that you'd like to be working in and progress, either or both.

Where are your customers based? Market/s?

....
....
....
....
....

What are the demographics of these countries?

....
....
....
....
....

Who exactly are your customers?

....
....
....
....
....

What percentage of your company/sector's customer base is female and what is the age range?

....
....
....
....
....

Now, look at the company you are working for or with, if you have your business: what is the employee's ratio of males to females?

....
....
....
....
....

What is the percentage of women in middle management and in leadership positions?

....
....
....
....
....

How does it compare to the percentage of men in middle management and in leadership positions?

....
....
....
....
....

How does this relate to your sector/company customer base ratio of male to females (I hope you see where I am going here…)?

....
....
....
....
....

Is your company male to female ratio at different levels or reflective of your market/s and customer base?

....
....
....

In February 2017 UN Women, a division of the United Nations dedicated to gender equality and the empowerment of women, unveiled The "Roadmap for Substantive Equality: 2030", in line with and supportive of the concerted global efforts to achieve the 2030 Agenda for Sustainable Development.

The purpose of the Roadmap is to repeal and/or amend discriminatory laws against women whilst ensuring that laws are supportive in general of gender equality & women's human rights.

The UN Women Roadmap for Substantive Equality: 2030 focuses not only in achieving legislative reform but equally, and more crucially, that they are put into practice.

The move from theory to practice, from the legislative framework to roll out and enforcement will require global coordination among different types of international and regional organizations, governments and so on.

The current estimate is that around 90% of the countries worldwide have at least one or more discriminatory law in their legislative framework with many different examples not exclusive to gender pay gap or women in leadership but also failures to adequately tackle violence against women, sexual harassment in public spaces and participation in politics. Gender-discriminatory laws are often rooted in discriminatory social norms, which remain pervasive and are difficult to change.

Action Point

List current social norms you believe to be discriminatory.

....
....
....
....
....
....
....
....
....
....
....
....
....
....
....
....
....
....
....
....
....
....
....
....
....

Great job!

3 things to be thankful for

Think back at the topic covered today — what are the 3 things you are grateful for, despite everything? Remember, if you can't think of any — you are not looking hard enough. Think again.

....
....
....
....
....
....
....
....
....
....
....
....
....
....
....
....
....
....
....
....
....
....
....
....
....
....

DAY 3: ONCE UPON A TIME

The Monkey Mind/dump the c*** exercise

Prompt:

What is a woman's place?

....
....
....
....
....
....
....
....
....
....
....
....
....
....

A woman's place

What a "woman's place" is or seen to be has varied throughout history from warriors, powerful priestesses, and political leaders to portrayals inferior to men and I think looking briefly, very briefly (I'm not going to bore you with history and a historical portrait — it was not the purpose of the book and less than less this workbook) at the position of women at different points in history it can show us how our society has grown and changed and help us to understand the present, including barriers.

Women have gained and lost power at different times in history; if we look at back at the early times in Christian church, women could hold positions of influence equal to men, (even though the Da Vinci Code is a work of fiction, there are indications that Mary Magdalene was once a significant religious leader — an apocryphal gospel of Mary Magdalene was discovered in the late nineteenth century in Egypt – having a gospel in itself is of significance here).

The fourth and fifth centuries AD, however, saw the degrading of women in the writings of people such as Tertullian, Saint Augustine and Saint Jerome blaming Eve, and consequently by association all women, for the downfall of humanity.

The late 1500s is generally seen as the beginning of Modern History with the Renaissance. Yes, women were painted and portrayed beautifully, but this did not really affect women on a day-to-day basis.

A woman's place was defined as the homemaker with strict expectations: women could not vote and were discouraged in owning a business.

. . .

Women of aristocratic families (with properties) were often forced/offered into political marriages where all their property then transferred to their husband.

The biggest gains in equality had to wait until the twentieth century, for example, with the Suffragettes successful campaign for women being granted the right to vote. World War one and two also showed that women could contribute to the economy and could work both inside and outside the home, taking men's places in factories.

The sixties and seventies and the advent of feminism further changed some of society's perceptions and, most importantly changed women's own beliefs.

Action point

Think back at three distinctive times in history — your choice: what was a woman's place in those times?

....

....

....

....

....

....

....

....

....

....

....

....

....

....

What did those beliefs mean for/translate to for women?

....
....
....
....
....

Find at least three heroines in those times that succeeded despite those negative perceptions/barriers:

....
....
....
....
....

What set them apart?

....
....
....
....
....

Shorter day today, good job.

3 things to be thankful for

Think back at the topic covered today — what are the 3 things you are grateful for, despite everything? Remember, if you can't think of any — you are not looking hard enough. Think again.

....
....
....
....
....
....
....
....
....
....
....
....
....
....
....
....
....
....
....
....
....
....
....
....
....

DAY 4: WHAT ARE YOUR BARRIERS - PART 1

The Monkey Mind/dump the c*** exercise

Prompt:

What comes to mind when you hear the word barrier?

....
....
....
....
....
....
....
....
....
....
....
....
....
....

Cultural, religious & family paradigms

It is difficult to talk about religion without insulting/annoying someone somewhere and without being disputed on the interpretation/miss-interpretation of the scripture/s and this section is not meant in any way to be a pontification of the good/evil in religion/s and or the ultimate guide to mainstream religions' s views on women.

This section is to recognize and acknowledge that religion has played/is playing and will continue to play a big part in the way different groups of people perceive themselves and others and their definition of "what good looks like" including women and their role in society and that there is a correlation between the two.

Many religions share the same characterizations and expectations of a traditional female role:

- Raise and teach children,
- Maintain a Godly household,
- Assist the husband decisions,
- Retain and care for family & familial assets.

I'm not saying that religion is the problem but mainly one of the potential restrictions. Sexism, misogyny and patriarchy and attitudes exist often entangled with other social and political factors and ways of thinking, including religion.

When I say patriarchy I mean a system of power relations between men and women, where men and women are complicit and agential, and which privileges particular kinds of gender and sexual identities (usually heterosexual men) over others. These power relations are part of the inner structural personal system with your entire personal image built on this — your belief foundation — which determines what you believe you can and cannot do, how should you do it and why.

Action Point

Now is the time to take stock and look back, not to judge and/or recrimi-nate but to understand and then move on: what effect do you think your own cultural background, religion and family paradigms had including your own reaction to those and how have they limited you-if they did that is (I know these are sensitive subjects, nevertheless, like an addict, it is time to face reality).

Be honest (yes, you need to do some work here :-)).

....
....
....
....
....
....
....
....
....
....
....
....
....
....
....
....
....
....
....
....
....
....
....
....

For women who wish to have children, there are also the obviously added barriers of going through the gestation period, the birth and consequent time needed to care for a newborn and beyond.

There is the physical barrier (not everyone has an easy pregnancy and is able to continue to perform to the same level/with the same intensity — the time-off pre/post — part) together with the childcare requirements.

Society is made of tribal congregations (religious and secular institutions, communities and families) all with their individual, sometimes divergent and sometimes mutually supportive views of a "woman's place", a "mother's duty" and "the right way of doing things".

Action Point

What are your inherited views about motherhood and a "mother's duty"?

....
....
....
....
....
....
....
....
....
....
....
....
....
....
....

Are these views supportive or conflicting with your desire for professional success and climbing the ladder? How so?

....
....
....
....
....
....
....
....
....
....
....
....
....
....
....
....
....
....
....
....
....
....
....
....

Gosh, that was heavy - You need a break for today.

3 things to be thankful for

Think back at the topic covered today — what are the 3 things you are grateful for, despite everything? Remember, if you can't think of any — you are not looking hard enough. Think again.

....

....

....

....

....

....

....

....

....

....

....

....

....

....

....

....

....

....

....

....

....

....

....

....

DAY 5: WHAT ARE YOUR BARRIERS - PART 2

The Monkey Mind/dump the c*** exercise

Prompt:

What comes to mind when you hear the words "good girl"?

....
....
....
....
....
....
....
....
....
....
....
....
....
....
....

The "good girl syndrome"

Although there is definitely the outer game of society/family paradigms and so on, there is also a far more important inner game, your own perceptions, your own decisions, belief systems that drive behavior and choices made — the "good girl syndrome".

Rachida Dati comes to mind, the French Justice Minister under French President Nicolas Sarkozy who went back to work five days after having her first child by Caesarean section. Seeing her going back as what is perceived (by whom?) too soon started a barrage and ping-pong of comments and articles, some quite bitching and derogative and some alleging bullying from Sarkozy (and the worse ones were from women).

Even the way she was described ("impossibly glamorous and thin") had negative connotations (like what-all new mothers must look/are fat and frumpy??).

Better still, people were discussing if she is *right to put the demands of her career ahead of her child? Or is she crazy to miss out on some of the most precious months of her life?* " like there is only one way of being a mother AND a career woman at the same time.

Action Point

How much have your cultural/religious and family paradigms conditioned your views on what a "good girl" behaves like?

....
....
....

How much has it affected your career aspirations and/or choices?

....
....
....
....
....
....
....
....
....
....
....
....
....
....
....
....
....
....
....
....
....
....
....
....

Short day today — great job.

3 things to be thankful for

Think back at the topic covered today — what are the 3 things you are grateful for, despite everything? Remember, if you can't think of any — you are not looking hard enough. Think again.

....
....
....
....
....
....
....
....
....
....
....
....
....
....
....
....
....
....
....
....
....
....
....
....
....

DAY 6: WHAT ARE YOUR BARRIERS - PART 3

The Monkey Mind/dump the c*** exercise

Prompt:

What comes to mind when you hear the words "bias"?

....
....
....
....
....
....
....
....
....
....
....
....
....
....
....

Who's a "good girl"?

Today we are going to delve deeper and this time into "your" idea of a "good girl".

Action point

Following from yesterday's exercises you should now have a good idea of your beliefs derived from the social/religious and family paradigms regarding the "good girl" syndrome (if you can't remember, go and take a look — go on .... I'll wait ;-)).

Now think back at times when you applied this "learnt judgement" and passed it onto others: go as far back or as near as you need to. Actually, I invite you to do so on purpose and see how and if your behavior changed with time.

Describe three different occasions at three different times in your life when you have demonstrated bias towards other women — or yourself — based on the learnt "good girl" syndrome belief (it is hard to admit, but we all do it and we all project our beliefs with our behavior — the point here is to have awareness).

....
....
....
....
....
....
....
....
....
....
....

....
....
....
....
....
....
....
....
....
....
....
....
....
....

How would you/could behave differently now, if the same situations arise again?

....
....
....
....
....
....
....
....
....
....
....

With understanding and acknowledging your own biases, you are taking step forward to a more level playing field — for yourself and other women. Congratulations.

3 things to be thankful for

Think back at the topic covered today — what are the 3 things you are grateful for, despite everything? Remember, if you can't think of any — you are not looking hard enough. Think again.

....

....

....

....

....

....

....

....

....

....

....

....

....

....

....

....

....

....

....

....

....

....

....

....

....

DAY 7: REST, RELAXATION AND SOME REFLECTION

The Monkey Mind/dump the c*** exercise

Prompt:
  Self-belief

....
....
....
....
....
....
....
....
....
....
....
....
....
....

This page is intentionally left blank

3 things to be thankful for

Think back at the topic covered today — what are the 3 things you are grateful for, despite everything? Remember, if you can't think of any — you are not looking hard enough. Think again.

....
....
....
....
....
....
....
....
....
....
....
....
....
....
....
....
....
....
....
....
....
....
....
....
....

DAY 8: REST, RELAXATION AND SOME REFLECTION

The Monkey Mind/dump the c*** exercise

Prompt:

Time for self

....
....
....
....
....
....
....
....
....
....
....
....
....
....

This page is intentionally left blank

3 things to be thankful for

Think back at the topic covered today — what are the 3 things you are grateful for, despite everything? Remember, if you can't think of any — you are not looking hard enough. Think again.

....
....
....
....
....
....
....
....
....
....
....
....
....
....
....
....
....
....
....
....
....
....
....
....
....

DAY 9: SUCCESS IS A RELATIVE THING - PART 1

*The Monkey Mind/dump the c*** exercise*

Prompt:

What comes to mind when you hear the word SUCCESS?

....
....
....
....
....
....
....
....
....
....
....
....
....
....
....

What does success mean to you?

Success means so many things to so many people; if you don't define what good (or great) looks like, you will be always chasing something, the next shiny object, unachievable targets and never be quite satisfied.

Action Point

Pause for a minute and think — jot down what is your definition of success.

....
....
....
....
....
....
....
....

Where does this definition originate from (family, friends, peers)?

....
....
....
....
....
....
....
....

Is this definition still relevant to you now? If yes (or no), why yes (or no)?

....
....
....
....
....
....
....

Has this definition changed in the last few years? If yes, what has changed?

....
....
....
....
....
....
....

What has been the constant (as compared to the variable) in your definition of success?

....
....
....
....
....
....

Well done.

3 things to be thankful for

Think back at the topic covered today — what are the 3 things you are grateful for, despite everything? Remember, if you can't think of any — you are not looking hard enough. Think again.

....
....
....
....
....
....
....
....
....
....
....
....
....
....
....
....
....
....
....
....
....
....
....
....
....

DAY 10: SUCCESS IS A RELATIVE THING - PART 2

The Monkey Mind/dump the c*** exercise

Prompt:

What do you feel when you hear the words GLASS CEILING?

....

....

....

....

....

....

....

....

....

....

....

....

....

....

What does success really mean to you?

Success means so many things to so many people; we have looked at what is your definition of success and how that has changed from a rational viewpoint. Now is the time to go deeper into your feelings.

Action point

Take some time to think about what success really means to you: a job well done? Position? Power?

....
....
....
....
....
....
....

How would you know you have arrived?

....
....
....
....
....
....
....

What is the feeling that success/THE job will give you?

....
....
....
....
....

What is really important to you:

- *Respect from colleagues / family / friends*
- *Financial security/money?*
- *Fulfilling expectations (family/friends/society)?*
- *Other?*

....
....
....
....
....
....
....

What is the destination and why? What will it give you?

....
....
....
....
....
....
....

What will make you feel truly successful?

....
....
....
....
....
....

How can you start feeling that now? Once you understand what success means to you, you can then recognize it and celebrate it — daily. Feeling successful, fulfilled breathes confidence — the more you recognize your achievements and feel good about them — the more confident you feel and the bigger things you will attempt, get my drift? ;-)

Great job.

3 things to be thankful for

Think back at the topic covered today — what are the 3 things you are grateful for, despite everything? Remember, if you can't think of any — you are not looking hard enough. Think again.

....
....
....
....
....
....
....
....
....
....
....
....
....
....
....
....
....
....
....
....
....
....
....
....
....

DAY 11: WHAT IS YOUR WHY?

The Monkey Mind/dump the c*** exercise

Prompt:

What do you need?

....
....
....
....
....
....
....
....
....
....
....
....
....
....

The Maslow Hierarchy of Needs

Maslow Hierarchy of Needs is one of the best-known motivational theories trying to understand what drives
"Humans".

Abraham Maslow, a human psychologist, explained this concept in his 1943 paper "A Theory of Human Motivation" and his subsequent book "Motivation and Personality" stating that our actions are motivated so to satisfy certain needs.

Maslow suggests that people are motivated to fulfill basic needs before moving on to the more advanced needs, trying to understand what makes people happy and the things that they do/would to fulfill their needs.

His belief was that people have an innate need and desire to be all they can be but to do so they must meet first a number of more basic needs (the most common representation of this theory is often a pyramid, moving from most basic needs at the bottom to the most complex at the top).

According to Maslow there are five different levels starting at the lowest known as physiological needs.

The bottom of the pyramid has the most basic physical require-ments including the need for food, water, sleep, and warmth, and once these are satisfied and people progress up the pyramid, and then these become more and more psychological and social, and so on, all the way to self-actualization, e.g., growing and developing as a person in order to achieve own potential.

Physiological, security, social, and esteem needs are what we would call deficiency needs, arising from lack and satisfying them is important in order to avoid unpleasant situations.

On the other hand at the highest levels of the pyramid are growth needs, which do not stem from deprivation, but rather from a desire to grow as a person.

The need for security and safety then becomes primary and it is all about control and order in our lives and consequent behaviors (financial security, health and wellness, safety against accidents and injury).

The need for appreciation and respect, e.g., gaining the respect and appreciation of others leads to the need to accomplish things and then have efforts recognized together with the feeling of accomplishment and prestige, self-esteem and personal worth.

Self-actualization - "What a man can be, he must be", is the need people have to achieve their full potential as human beings.

"It may be loosely described as the full use and exploitation of talents, capabilities, potentialities, etc. Such people seem to be fulfilling themselves and to be doing the best that they are capable of doing... They are people who have developed or are developing to the full stature of which they are capable," Abraham Maslow.

Similarly to Maslow Tony Robbins, in his programs and many books, talks about in a more fluid & less hierarchical way the same drivers of human behaviors:

- Certainty and security
- Uncertainty and variety
- Significance
- Love & Connection
- Growth
- Contribution.

It is important here not to be too rigid about the standard progression of the needs within the pyramid: what is more important or indeed essential to one person might not be to others (except perhaps the basic physiological needs that are vital to our survival and essential to the survival and propagation of the species).

My point here is that, on top of the infrastructural belief system based on cultural, religious (or non-religious) & family paradigms, there are basic human needs that need to be fulfilled.

Action Point

This is a good time for a pause and to reflect: looking either at Maslow's pyramid or Tony Robbins's list which one/s of those need/s is/are the most important to you?

How are you fulfilling them right now?

....
....
....
....
....
....
....
....
....
....
....
....
....

What is your why (for that coveted glass/ceiling position)? Are you trying to satisfy your needs or responding to external expectations?

....
....
....
....
....
....
....
....
....
....
....
....
....
....
....

Refer back to your definition of success and what THE position/s would give you? Were you really honest (with yourself)?

....
....
....
....
....
....
....
....
....
....
....
....

You are doing great.

3 things to be thankful for

Think back at the topic covered today — what are the 3 things you are grateful for, despite everything? Remember, if you can't think of any — you are not looking hard enough. Think again.

....
....
....
....
....
....
....
....
....
....
....
....
....
....
....
....
....
....
....
....
....
....
....
....

DAY 12: WHAT IS THE PRICE?

The Monkey Mind/dump the c*** exercise

Prompt:

What is your price?

....
....
....
....
....
....
....
....
....
....
....
....
....
....
....

Everyone pays a price

There is a perception that women (even more so women with children) pay a price to rise to the top of an organization / field , etc., (as opposed to it is easy for men?).

Let's face it:

Leadership requires 100% commitment – Everyone pays a price.

Action Point

This point is really important: if the "price to pay" for success/the position is perceived as "too big/painful" and/or unfair, there will always be an invisible barrier, like a force field stopping you from getting there.

Take some time to think what would be the sacrifices you'd have to make to achieve the top positions/dream job , etc.

Are they real or perceived? And, most importantly, are you willing to make them?

....
....
....
....
....
....
....
....
....
....
....
....
....
....

....
....
....
....
....
....
....
....
....
....

Are you making them too big? Are you self-sabotaging? If yes, what are you scared of? No BS here, we are all scared of something, write down your fears.

OK, done?

STOP IT!

Stop making excuses, It is all B*****t.

In the 2015 Global Entrepreneurship Monitor (GEM) Special Report on Women Entrepreneurship, women's entrepreneurship rose by 6% worldwide in the last two years.

According to the 2016 Kauffman Index of Start-up Activity, in the United States women make up 40% of new entrepreneurs (highest since 1996). In the MasterCard Index of Women Entrepreneurs 2017 (MIWE) women's business ownership across the 54 markets measured make up between 25-35% of total business owners.

On Day 2 – *Where are you now* — we have seen the statistics on women on boardroom representation according to some recent reports (respectively 14,7% Credit Suisse, 15% Morgan Stanley and 12% Deloitte using different samples). The barriers are the same including childcare.

And on that note, I'll leave you to ponder...

3 things to be thankful for

Think back at the topic covered today — what are the 3 things you are grateful for, despite everything? Remember, if you can't think of any — you are not looking hard enough. Think again.

....
....
....
....
....
....
....
....
....
....
....
....
....
....
....
....
....
....
....
....
....
....
....
....
....
....

DAY 13: PERFECTION IS BORING - BE AWESOME INSTEAD

The Monkey Mind/dump the c*** exercise

Prompt:

What comes to mind when thinking of perfection?

....
....
....
....
....
....
....
....
....
....
....
....
....
....

Wonder Woman does not exist

The idea that you should take as little maternity leave as possible, work until your waters break beneath your desk, never complain of sickness, swollen ankles and/or backache, and then go back to work fast and/or go back to work and (as much as you love your baby and being a mum) enjoying being back to work and more than baby-talk, but feeling guilty all the way through it, and then coming back home and be the "perfect" wife/partner/significant other (whatever you like to be called) and cooking, cleaning, tidying and putting the baby to bed is ludicrous.

Silence your inner critic — do you and what works for you.

Action Point

Does the picture described above sound like someone you know? Maybe intimately? What are the things that you do to please your inner critic?

....
....
....
....
....
....
....
....
....
....
....
....
....
....
....
....

The practicality of looking after a child, and who is going to do it post return to work exists and unfortunately, no matter the progress made recently, we can't deny that women, in the vast majority of cases, still bear the burden of household and family responsibility. That means women in general and even more so women aspiring to leadership positions have to juggle even more than their male counterparts.

All the employment laws on maternity, paternity, shared parental leave and flexible working mean absolutely nothing unless men take up/opt for these opportunities and support their partner/wife/significant other. It is easy to criticize "society", the government, businesses , etc., and ask for more laws, more rules to aid women coming back to work and pursuing a career/leadership and talk about what "men should do more".

Society is made of families and individuals and the change will happen and can happen — starting from your family and your partner taking up a fair share of childcare/household duties and so on.

Relationships do break up sometime but this does not nullify paternal responsibilities and accountabilities in raising children irrespectively of how much you might dislike/hate/can't stand your ex-partner and their new life (of course there might be fathers/parents who are unfit although let's consider this for argument sake to be an exception than the rule).

Think of your family unit as a business with two main shareholders whereby the decisions made are for the best interest of the "business"/family unit whilst not stifling ambitions and/or disadvantage either and/or both shareholders.

Too many times men request flexible working and or parental leave (and/or maternity leave) only and exclusively when their wife/partner/significant other already earns more than they do, far more rarely when they are on equal earning footing or thereabouts .The discussion needs to happen about your mutual ambition and career aspiration together with shared responsibilities and potential support needed (in what forms and by whom).

True feminism means accepting both the reality of motherhood, and celebrating its real value personally and to society as a whole but also having equal opportunities and being able to make a choice on how you would like to deal with your career and motherhood without having to apologize if you are ambitious and want to go back to work as soon as, or take a few years off.

Action Point

This is the time to look inside your own relationship – I don't want to cause breakups, nevertheless you know what needs doing here...

....
....
....
....
....
....
....
....
....
....
....
....
....
....
....
....
....
....
....

3 things to be thankful for

Think back at the topic covered today — what are the 3 things you are grateful for, despite everything? Remember, if you can't think of any — you are not looking hard enough. Think again.

....
....
....
....
....
....
....
....
....
....
....
....
....
....
....
....
....
....
....
....
....
....
....
....
....
....

DAY 14: REST, RELAXATION AND SOME REFLECTION

The Monkey Mind/dump the c*** exercise

Prompt:

Forgiveness

....
....
....
....
....
....
....
....
....
....
....
....
....
....

This page is intentionally left blank

3 things to be thankful for

Think back at the topic covered today — what are the 3 things you are grateful for, despite everything? Remember, if you can't think of any — you are not looking hard enough. Think again.

....
....
....
....
....
....
....
....
....
....
....
....
....
....
....
....
....
....
....
....
....
....
....
....
....

DAY 15: REST, RELAXATION AND SOME REFLECTION

The Monkey Mind/dump the c*** exercise

Prompt:

Self-respect

....
....
....
....
....
....
....
....
....
....
....
....
....
....

This page is intentionally left blank

3 things to be thankful for

Think back at the topic covered today — what are the 3 things you are grateful for, despite everything? Remember, if you can't think of any — you are not looking hard enough. Think again.

....
....
....
....
....
....
....
....
....
....
....
....
....
....
....
....
....
....
....
....
....
....
....
....
....
....

DAY 16: THINK OUTSIDE THE BOX: WHAT BOX? LOOK THE PART

The Monkey Mind/dump the c*** exercise

Prompt:

First Impressions

....
....
....
....
....
....
....
....
....
....
....
....
....
....

The power of first impressions

According to Malcolm Gladwell, in "Blink: The Power of Thinking Without Thinking" people make up their minds about people they meet for the first time instantaneously or in two-seconds — can you imagine?!

Research also suggests that first impressions can be so powerful that they can become more important and believable than fact.

Recent studies presented at the Society of Personality and Social Psychology annual conference in Texas found that even when told whether a person was gay or straight, people identified a person's sexual orientation based on how they looked — irrespectively of the facts blatantly contradicting their impression.

"We judge books by their covers, and we can't help but do it," said Nicholas Rule, PhD, of the University of Toronto. "With effort, we can overcome this to some extent, but we are continually tasked with needing to correct ourselves."

"Furthermore, the less time we have to make our judgments, the more likely we are to go with our gut, even over fact.

As soon as one sees another person, an impression is formed. This happens so quickly that what we see can sometimes dominate what we know," Rule said.

Additionally, the first impression formed online is often more negative than a first impression formed in person.

. . .

Action point

Think back at least two occasions when you made assumptions about people you had just met based on their appearance: let's start with your private life.

....
....
....
....
....
....
....
....
....
....
....
....
....
....

How did you behave with those people based on your initial assumptions?

....
....
....
....
....
....
....
....
....
....
....
....
....
....

Did your behavior change once you got to know them? How?

....
....
....
....
....
....
....
....
....
....
....
....
....
....
....

Now let's repeat exactly the full exercise with your professional life. If you think you have never done so, think again — we ALL do it and so have you.

....
....
....
....
....
....
....
....
....
....
....
....
....
....
....

Ok, to finish for the day, let's look back when other people have made assumptions about yourself and treated you a certain way (which?) because of those assumptions (pick an example from your personal life or professional life — either, both and go as deep as you wish). How did it make you feel?

....

....

....

....

....

....

....

....

....

....

....

....

....

....

....

....

....

....

....

....

....

....

....

....

....

....

....

Can you recognize where these biases are coming from? Might be worth revisiting previous week/s exercises here, just saying ;-)...

....
....
....
....
....
....
....
....
....
....
....
....
....
....
....
....
....
....
....
....
....
....
....
....
....
....
....
....

Great job.

3 things to be thankful for

Think back at the topic covered today — what are the 3 things you are grateful for, despite everything? Remember, if you can't think of any — you are not looking hard enough. Think again.

....
....
....
....
....
....
....
....
....
....
....
....
....
....
....
....
....
....
....
....
....
....
....
....
....
....

DAY 17: THINK OUTSIDE THE BOX: WHAT BOX? LOOK THE PART

*The Monkey Mind/dump the c*** exercise*

Prompt:

Perceptions

....
....
....
....
....
....
....
....
....
....
....
....
....
....

The Halo effect

First impressions do matter for both good and bad depending if the first meeting was fine or not — positive = social cohesion; negative = potential biases and social prejudice — like a halo effect.

Our appearance makes an instant statement to others about who we are and what we are about.

I know that, when this subject is approached, women especially get all uppity saying appearance doesn't matter, shouldn't matter, blah blah blah …

I get it. It shouldn't. It does.

Additionally, the impression created by appearance further influences our judgement, creating the so-called halo effect.

What is the halo effect then?

It is a cognitive bias whereby the overall impression we have of a person affects how we feel and think about their character, e.g., you see someone in a similar light of your perception of one characteristic for all others.

For example, in a work setting, the halo effect is one of the most common biases affecting performance appraisals and reviews.

It also has an impact on how severely or lightly we perceive and judge mistakes.

For example, when someone that we perceive to be a "good guy/girl" makes a mistake, we tend to minimize the error "it's a one off"; "he/she might be going through something...".

· · ·

On the contrary, when someone that we perceive as "not good" makes an error, then boy oh boy, " he/she always makes mistakes", "again? I knew it..." and so on.

Action point

Go back to the exercises done yesterday now: did those initial impressions in your private life create a halo effect in consequent interactions? If yes, how? Describe what happened. If not, are you sure, really sure? I thought so.

....
....
....
....
....
....
....
....
....
....
....
....
....
....
....
....
....
....
....
....
....
....
....
....
....
....

Now think back to examples when you have "applied" the halo effect in the workplace based on your perceptions and over-reacted or under-reacted to people based on this. Positive examples first: when did you underplay work errors/mistakes because of your overall opinion of the person/s? Be honest here.

....
....
....
....
....
....
....
....
....
....
....
....
....
....
....
....
....
....
....
....
....
....
....
....
....
....
....
....

Ok, now negative examples, when you overreacted to errors/mistakes (which you wouldn't have if the same errors came from "the good people"). Don't beat yourself up, we all do it. Recognizing own biases is the first step to beat them.

....
....
....
....
....
....
....
....
....
....
....
....
....
....
....
....
....
....
....
....
....
....
....
....
....

Great job.

3 things to be thankful for

Think back at the topic covered today — what are the 3 things you are grateful for, despite everything? Remember, if you can't think of any — you are not looking hard enough. Think again.

....
....
....
....
....
....
....
....
....
....
....
....
....
....
....
....
....
....
....
....
....
....
....
....
....
....

DAY 18: THINK OUTSIDE THE BOX: WHAT BOX? LOOK THE PART

*The Monkey Mind/dump the c*** exercise*

Prompt:

Snob

....
....
....
....
....
....
....
....
....
....
....
....
....
....

A book and its cover

Appearance does matter and it does with people in the same way that it does with products.

Manufacturing is one very good example of this.

Many times factories produce consumer goods that have the exact same recipe/product specification but, at the end of the production line, different labels are applied.

The products are then perceived/received in a completely different manner by consumers (including sometimes a substantial price point difference).

This is both because of the perception of quality (based on the branding/marketing of the different labels/brands) but also what buying certain brands says about us and how we want to be seen.

Think about that.

Action point

Make a list of the places where you habitually shop: what are the key components of their brand? What do they have in common?

....
....
....
....
....
....
....
....
....
....
....
....
....
....
....

Why do you shop there, be specific. What does it say about you as a consumer and as a person? How does that make you feel?

....
....
....
....
....
....
....
....
....
....
....
....
....

List all the shops you'd never be seen dead in: why is that? What are your associations with those brands? What do you think it says about people who shop there? Honesty is the key here — this is your workbook and nobody will see it unless you share it — challenge your perceptions.

....
....
....
....
....
....
....
....
....
....
....
....
....
....

Let's talk products now: are there any brands that you are particularly attached to — emotionally? Why are you attached to them?

....
....
....
....
....
....
....
....
....
....
....
....

I know right now you don't believe me, challenge yourself to carry out blind tests on five different types of products from branded houses and super-market own labels. Make it a game with your friend and challenge your perceptions. Go on, you know you want to …

What were the results?

....
....
....
....
....
....
....
....
....
....
....
....

Learned anything today then? I thought so ;-)

3 things to be thankful for

Think back at the topic covered today — what are the 3 things you are grateful for, despite everything? Remember, if you can't think of any — you are not looking hard enough. Think again.

....
....
....
....
....
....
....
....
....
....
....
....
....
....
....
....
....
....
....
....
....
....
....
....
....
....
....

DAY 19: THINK OUTSIDE THE BOX: WHAT BOX? LOOK THE PART

The Monkey Mind/dump the c*** exercise

Prompt:

Women in leadership

....
....
....
....
....
....
....
....
....
....
....
....
....
....

Leading Lady - Part 1

Personal style goes way beyond clothes and can also be used to communicate and reinforce your message.

"Style is a way to say who you are
without having to speak."
- Rachel Zoe

Today we are going to, well actually you are going to, look into exactly this:
understanding what you are saying to the world.

Having knowledge about yourself and how you come across will enable you to create a personal style that goes beyond clothes and encompasses your approach to your career and life and how you feel about yourself.

Action Point

Describe your personal style — what are the words that come to mind?

....
....
....
....
....
....
....
....
....
....
....

What are the words that other people would use instead to describe your personal style? What do you think your style says about you? Are you aware of what are you projecting right now?

....
....
....
....
....
....
....
....
....
....
....
....
....

How does this contribute to the perception people might have of you (feel free to go back to previous days exercises if you need some help with this)?

....
....
....
....
....
....
....
....
....
....
....
....
....

How aligned is your current personal style to your career (and/or personal) aspirations?

....
....
....
....
....
....
....
....
....
....
....
....
....
....
....
....
....
....
....
....
....
....
....
....
....
....

Good job.

3 things to be thankful for

Think back at the topic covered today — what are the 3 things you are grateful for, despite everything? Remember, if you can't think of any — you are not looking hard enough. Think again.

....

....

....

....

....

....

....

....

....

....

....

....

....

....

....

....

....

....

....

....

....

....

....

....

....

DAY 20: THINK OUTSIDE THE BOX: WHAT BOX? LOOK THE PART

The Monkey Mind/dump the c*** exercise

Prompt:

Fashion

....
....
....
....
....
....
....
....
....
....
....
....
....
....

Leading Lady - Part 2

> *"Real style is never right or wrong.*
> *It's a matter of being yourself on purpose."*
> **- G. Bruce Brier**

Personal style goes way beyond clothes and can also be used to communicate and reinforce your message.

Yesterday we looked at your current personal style and what your appearance says about you.

Today we are going to have some fun and create a Mood Board.

A **Mood Board** is a type of visual presentation or "collage" consisting of images, text, and samples of objects in a composition to convey a general idea or feeling about a particular topic. The topic, on this occasion, is the style of women you admire that appeal to you that you resonate with.

Action point

Look at magazines, Pinterest, Instagram, or wherever you can find inspiration, and put together a so-called **Mood Board** for looks that you like.

Personally I like physical things and keep them handy; you might want to do the same, as they'll be useful next week. I left a blank page so you can attach/pin "stuff". Have fun :-)

This page is intentionally left blank

3 things to be thankful for

Think back at the topic covered today — what are the 3 things you are grateful for, despite everything? Remember, if you can't think of any — you are not looking hard enough. Think again.

....

....

....

....

....

....

....

....

....

....

....

....

....

....

....

....

....

....

....

....

....

....

....

....

....

DAY 21: REST, RELAXATION AND SOME REFLECTION

*The Monkey Mind/dump the c*** exercise*

Prompt:

Style

....
....
....
....
....
....
....
....
....
....
....
....
....
....

This page is intentionally left blank

3 things to be thankful for

Think back at the topic covered today — what are the 3 things you are grateful for, despite everything? Remember, if you can't think of any — you are not looking hard enough. Think again.

....

....

....

....

....

....

....

....

....

....

....

....

....

....

....

....

....

....

....

....

....

....

....

....

....

DAY 22: REST, RELAXATION AND SOME REFLECTION

The Monkey Mind/dump the c*** exercise

Prompt:

My personal style

....
....
....
....
....
....
....
....
....
....
....
....
....
....

This page is intentionally left blank

3 things to be thankful for

Think back at the topic covered today — what are the 3 things you are grateful for, despite everything? Remember, if you can't think of any — you are not looking hard enough. Think again.

....
....
....
....
....
....
....
....
....
....
....
....
....
....
....
....
....
....
....
....
....
....
....
....
....

DAY 23: THINK OUTSIDE THE BOX: WHAT BOX? LOOK THE PART

The Monkey Mind/dump the c*** exercise

Prompt:

Fashion icons

....
....
....
....
....
....
....
....
....
....
....
....
....
....

If you want to be the best, you need to learn from the best – I have not invented this phrase — you can hear it for the lips of the most successful entrepreneurs, CEOs, billionaires out there. And that is the point.

> *"If you want to be successful,*
> *find someone who has achieved the results you want*
> *and copy what they do*
> *and you'll achieve the same results."*
> **- Tony Robbins**

You need someone who has been there, seen it, done it and got the t-shirt so to speak and you can emulate exactly what he or she has done and shortcut your way to success.

This is applicable to both people you associate with on a daily basis and to choosing mentors to speed your journey, and includes the personal/work style department.

Today we are going to look at two fashion icons and how they used their personal style/appearance to communicate and reinforce their message: Jackie Kennedy Onassis and Diana, Princess of Wales.

I can picture your horrified faces right now reading this: Laura what? R-E-A-L-L-Y???

. . .

Yes, really (hey, I could have said the Queen, but that was pushing it a bit far perhaps ...).

So, why Jackie Kennedy and Diana, Princess of Wales?

Firstly, both women have been photographed ad infinitum and it will be easy for you to carry out the exercises. Secondly, and most importantly, these are two women who were thrown into the public eye and have adapted their style to the specific situation to convey a message FOR that specific situation whilst remaining true to themselves and their "persona", on and off duty.

Two examples come to mind (but you can find endless):

- Jackie Kennedy wearing red, paying diplomatic tribute to the host country on her visit to Canada, and
- Diana wearing her "revenge" dress on the very night Prince Charles was making his adultery admission in a tell-all TV interview.

Diana evolved her style more and more through the years, and particularly so after her divorce, leaving beyond royal restrictions and protocols — a perfect example on how anyone can morph their style and re-invent themselves.

Both used clothes as self-expression and a means to communicate. And so can you.

> *"Dress like you are going to meet*
> *your worst enemy today."*
> **- Coco Chanel**

Action point

Describe in your own words both women's style: what words come to mind and why?

....

....

....

....

....

....

....

....

....

....

....

....

....

....

How did they make people feel? Be specific: how, why...

....

....

....

....

....

....

....

....

....

....

....

....

....

....

Observe their style evolution throughout the years — what are the key points that stayed the same and what changed?

....
....
....
....
....
....
....
....
....
....
....
....
....
....

Pick three key pieces/looks for both women that were particularly significant for the purpose of the exercise, e.g., communicating through clothes: which one did you pick and why?

....
....
....
....
....
....
....
....
....
....
....
....
....
....

Think back at previous weeks' exercises: your definition of success and what it really means to you. Based on your answers, what does success physically look like for you (and I do mean visualize THAT image of success): what style/clothes do you associate it with?

....
....
....
....
....
....
....
....
....
....
....
....

What lessons can you apply to yourself from both women in creating an effective personal style aligned and supportive to your personal career ambitions/idea of success?

....
....
....
....
....
....
....
....
....
....
....
....

That's it for today, good job.

3 things to be thankful for

Think back at the topic covered today — what are the 3 things you are grateful for, despite everything? Remember, if you can't think of any — you are not looking hard enough. Think again.

....
....
....
....
....
....
....
....
....
....
....
....
....
....
....
....
....
....
....
....
....
....
....
....
....

DAY 24: THINK OUTSIDE THE BOX: WHAT BOX? LOOK THE PART

*The Monkey Mind/dump the c*** exercise*

Prompt:

Role models

....
....
....
....
....
....
....
....
....
....
....
....
....
....

In every story, every hero is helped through his/her journey when meeting a mentor and then allies along the way.

Virtual or "real" mentors/allies/role models to show you their "call to adventure', their crossing of thresholds together with perhaps tests, allies and maybe enemies.

In this case we are building from yesterday's exercises and looking at other successful women who can be your role model to bring to life the "Look The Part" methodology and help you along the way to create/evolve your personal style into your own personal armour to conquer your career (and personal) goals.

> *"Create your own style ... let it be unique for yourself*
> *and yet identifiable for others."*
> **- Anna Wintour**

Action point

Let's go and find these women: look both in the public eye, in professional organizations, in your company and so on. Women who have done it and are living their life on their terms whilst representing their company at the highest level.

....
....
....
....
....
....
....

From the list, choose at least three and plan how you can target and maximize your learning — for example key looks during key moments in their career/for their company — how did they represent the company brand and assert themselves via their clothes/style?

....
....
....
....
....
....
....
....
....
....
....
....
....
....
....
....
....
....
....
....
....
....

"The process of growth,
of being an independent person,
of learning who you are and what you want from life,
is the real secret of life, happiness, and beauty ...
A fulfilled woman is a beautiful woman."
- Diane von Furstenberg

3 things to be thankful for

Think back at the topic covered today — what are the 3 things you are grateful for, despite everything? Remember, if you can't think of any — you are not looking hard enough. Think again.

....
....
....
....
....
....
....
....
....
....
....
....
....
....
....
....
....
....
....
....
....
....
....
....

DAY 25: THINK OUTSIDE THE BOX: WHAT BOX? LOOK THE PART

*The Monkey Mind/dump the c*** exercise*

Prompt:

Self-analysis

....
....
....
....
....
....
....
....
....
....
....
....
....
....

All together now

Now is the time to look back at the journey for the past three weeks or so, crystalize the learning so we can move into the fun part — building your new/evolved brand.

Action point

Describe your journey for the past three weeks — the good, the bad and the ugly.

....
....
....
....
....
....
....
....
....
....
....
....
....
....

What was the lowest point and why?

....
....
....
....
....
....

What was the highest point and why?

....
....
....
....
....
....
....
....

What have you learned about yourself?

....
....
....
....
....
....
....
....

What do you really (REALLY) want to achieve — the ultimate goal?

....
....
....
....
....
....
....
....

Why do you want it? What will give you?

....
....
....
....
....
....
....
....
....

What is your definition of success?

....
....
....
....
....
....
....
....
....

What does success look like to you? Describe the look and feel of success.

....
....
....
....
....
....
....
....
....

What price, if any, are you willing to pay to achieve your definition of success?

....
....
....
....
....
....
....
....
....
....
....
....
....
....

What are the barriers you have faced/are facing to achieve your goal and how are you going to tackle them now?

....
....
....
....
....
....
....
....
....
....
....
....
....

To what extent do you think your current personal brand (and the conse-quent impression of you people have) was a barrier to achieve "success"? Better still, how aligned is your current personal brand with your idea of "success" (I'm assuming there is some kind of disconnect between the two or you wouldn't have picked up this workbook in the first place)?

....
....
....
....
....
....
....
....
....
....
....
....
....
....

Write down key learning points from reviewing Jackie Kennedy and Diana, Princess of Wales style and communication through their appear-ance/clothes , etc.

....
....
....
....
....
....
....
....
....
....

Write down key learning points from looking at the style of other successful women and their style through key times in their career.

....
....
....
....
....
....
....
....
....
....
....
....
....
....
....
....
....
....
....
....
....
....
....
....
....
....
....
....
....
....

Great job.

3 things to be thankful for

Think back at the topic covered today — what are the 3 things you are grateful for, despite everything? Remember, if you can't think of any — you are not looking hard enough. Think again.

....
....
....
....
....
....
....
....
....
....
....
....
....
....
....
....
....
....
....
....
....
....
....
....
....
....

DAY 26: THINK OUTSIDE THE BOX: WHAT BOX? LOOK THE PART

The Monkey Mind/dump the c*** exercise

Prompt:

Personal brand

....
....
....
....
....
....
....
....
....
....
....
....
....
....

Brand You: identifying what makes you different

To live well, get what you want, whilst being satisfied along the way, you need to know how to present and sell yourself — emphasize your qualities, gloss over the not so good sides.

We have gone through this concept but I will go over it again, with a new analogy this time: between two windows with the same objects, one well done, the other without inventiveness, we stop decisively in front of the first.

A well-defined, memorable brand is essential:

- To help customers (bosses / clients etc.) remember the product (YOU)
- To convey a simple message quickly
- To help customers distinguishing the product (YOU) from similar products (other people)
- To create a positive appeal to entice someone to buy the product (offer you a position / promotion / funding).

The good news is you can help people to see you exactly as you would like them to with a well-defined personal brand.

"You Personal Style (Brand) melds your lifestyle, finances, and identity into an overall fashion statement that makes you feel good about yourself and tells the world how to feel about you ...
Getting the looks part out of the way allows you to get down to business and the true priorities of your life."
- Suzy Gershman

A personal brand will help you in standing out in a crowded arena and get noticed, whilst targeting your ideal customers (e.g., company / bosses / investors , etc.). Truth be said, you already have a personal brand (people's perception of you) and so far — as we have ascertained — this has not served you as well as it could have. Time to change it.

Action point

Let's work together in creating/evolving your personal brand.

First thing: making a list of adjectives that describe you physically, personality wise and other characteristics. Write down as many as you can think of in each column (I wrote some examples for you to start you off); they can be both positive AND negative.

Take your time and be specific.

Physical appearance	Personality traits	Additional
Example: brunette	*adventurous*	*Irish.*

Now that you have a full list it's time to do some "market research" e.g. find out how other people would describe you.

I would pick a mix of friends, family, co-workers (men and women). Ask them to be open and honest and do assure them that you would not take offense (please don't — remember they are already describing you THAT way when people ask them about you — you might as well know it).

Same drill as you did yourself:

Physical appearance	Personality traits	Additional
Example: brunette	*adventurous*	*Irish.*

This exercise will be very useful for tomorrow — good job!

DAY 27: THINK OUTSIDE THE BOX: WHAT BOX? LOOK THE PART

*The Monkey Mind/dump the c*** exercise*

Prompt:

Self-analysis

....
....
....
....
....
....
....
....
....
....
....
....
....
....

Creating your new personal brand

Presentation and selling are arts: there is definitely a dose of talent but also some professionalism that can be learned.

To present and sell yourself better, you need to know yourself well. That is, to evaluate the quality or the essential qualities on which to build a kingdom.

Needless to say personality wins, that mix of pleasant or unpleasant qualities that make an individual a person. Give yourself a sign that distinguishes you.

It must not be an "a solo" but a symphony in which a solo instrument plays the base. The same quality played on all the times is overwhelming, it wows when pulled out at the right moment.

Bluff very little and love yourself very much: don't invent "from scratch" features that you are far from possessing.

The right comparison is with actors. Each actor looks for his/her genre, then with time and experience, maybe he/she changes or integrates it. Or get good enough to recite any text as long as he/she cares.

However, when you decide what you want to bet on, get used to thinking of yourself as a person of that type. In short, enter the part until it is spontaneous and natural.

Beware of the most common mistakes:

- Haste - makes you lose sight of the goal
- Excess - never be too much. To be respected (and admired)

you have to give yourself a human image, with small shadow areas that highlight and brighten qualities

- Sectorialization - once you get into character, don't abandon it. You are not bluffing; you are just working on your personality. It makes no sense to have a public and a private image. Your project is and must be a total immersion project.

For this project (your new brand/personal style), it is essential to choose a field of action, a field of intervention and what I mean by this, is to identify clearly what you want to achieve (what is the position, in what sector/company, what level, what success looks like) because this is the starting point (hence all the exercises we have gone through in the past days).

Action point

In yesterday's exercises you compiled a list of different adjectives/words that you think describe your persona and also you should have asked other people to do the same. Now it is time to review all the data gathered — are there any commonalities? Any surprises?

....
....
....
....
....
....
....
....
....
....
....
....

*Select just three words/phrases from the overall data that make you **different**: a unique set of three positive attributes that together create an **interesting & attractive** personal brand.*

The criteria:

1. *The brand must ring true to who you are, both from your perspective but also <u>as others see you</u>*
2. *The brand has a wide appeal (don't niche down too much)*
3. *The brand is easy to remember and unique*
4. *The brand positions you for the role/company at the level you are aiming at.*

The selection of the three attributes, when combined, will make you stand out positively.

....

....

....

....

How the three attributes/words are combined will be the key to a standout personal brand, starting with "looking the part".

*Let's start with looking back at your mood board, your images of what success "looks like", examples of how Jackie Kennedy/Diana, Princess of Wales and the other successful women you admire communicate through their personal style. Select amongst all the images/examples the most aligned and representative of your **new** chosen brand (add more images if you need to) and create <u>the New YOU mood board.</u>*

· · ·

This page is left intentionally blank so you can stick all your pictures there, ready for the next two days - I know, I know, normally the weekend is for rest and relaxation, not this one. I want to make sure that, by the end of the workbook, you are ready to "Look The Part".

3 things to be thankful for

Think back at the topic covered today — what are the 3 things you are grateful for, despite everything? Remember, if you can't think of any — you are not looking hard enough. Think again.

....

....

....

....

....

....

....

....

....

....

....

....

....

....

....

....

....

....

....

....

....

....

....

....

DAY 28: NO REST FOR THE WICKED - WARDROBE CLEAN OUT

The Monkey Mind/dump the c*** exercise

Prompt:

Clothes and hoarding

....
....
....
....
....
....
....
....
....
....
....
....
....

The purpose of this weekend is to review your current wardrobe: get rid of excess and inappropriate clothing (for your new brand) and design a small, basic wardrobe that will look attractive and appropriate for all your lifestyle/business activities whilst being totally aligned with your new personal style/brand.

Remember the analogy with actors: once into character...

It makes no sense to have a public and a private image. Your project is and must be a total immersion project.

Ready to rock?

Action point

To start with, I'd suggest wearing good underwear (bear with me) and something comfy that it is easy to take off and on. Then gather some rubbish/recycling bags and cleaning materials (again, bear with me ...).

Now, empty your wardrobe/s and drawers — completely — and start cleaning

(let's face it, when was the last time you deep cleaned them?).

Yup, that's right — when you finish today you want a clean and fresh space for the "New YOU" clothes to be in.

Ok, go....

....
....
....
....
....
....
....

Cleaning done?

Now, look carefully at the pile of clothes on your bed/floor, wherever you put them ...

Look at them mercilessly, e.g., if they look tatty, raggedy it is time to take them to their rightful resting place, the clothes cemetery a.k.a. the recycling bin (not to charity).

Go on, this is where one of those recycling bags will come handy ...

....
....
....
....
....
....
....
....
....
....
....
....
....
....
....
....
....
....

Done? I shall refrain from asking how many bags, your secret is safe ;-)

And now the fun begins.

•   •   •

Let's pretend you are out shopping somewhere really fancy, get yourself a nice glass of wine (or a cup of tea if you prefer) and now you are going to try on E-V-E-R-Y-T-H-I-N-G they/you have in the shop, a.k.a. your clothes on the floor.

Be honest, objective and look not only how they sit on you but also how they make you feel: sexy? Powerful? Young? Frumpy?

As you are trying them on, divide the clothes in three piles:

1. *Fit just right*
2. *Too big*
3. *Too small.*

....
....
....
....
....
....
....
....
....
....
....
....
....
....
....
....

Done? Time for a quick comfort break ;-)

• • •

Now that you are back, you can put the clothes from **Pile 1** *(fit just right) back in the cleaned wardrobe that should be fully dry and smelling awesome by now. We will look at them again tomorrow.*

Pile 3 *(clothes too small — a.k.a. hanging on to the "dream"): if you were like the majority of women, including me, you'd probably have a collection (small or vast) of different sizes there.*

No judging, we have all done it. Now though is the time to be realistic.

Ask yourself a very simple question: am I committed to lose all the weight that I need in order to be able to fit into this size/these sizes again?

Only you know the answer to that question — my advice here would be to ditch anything smaller than one or two sizes at most (let's face it, if you were that way inclined and you really had wanted to, you would have by now).

Ok then, the discarded clothes are going into another recycling bag, ready for their new home: the charity shop. Leave the remaining clothes, if any, on one side for now.

Pile 2 *(clothes too big — a.k.a. the "just in case I put on weight again"): firstly, THIS has got to STOP! Not even going to attempt at being nice here.*

Secondly, these clothes could be boosting your existing wardrobe right now, with just a few modifications. But for now, you are going to put them neatly on a chair, ready for tomorrow, creating your capsule wardrobe for the "New YOU".

That's it for today; you deserve a medal (or a bottle of wine).

3 things to be thankful for

Think back at the topic covered today — what are the 3 things you are grateful for, despite everything? Remember, if you can't think of any — you are not looking hard enough. Think again.

....
....
....
....
....
....
....
....
....
....
....
....
....
....
....
....
....
....
....
....
....
....
....
....
....
....

DAY 29: NO REST OR RELAXATION - PUTTING IT ALL TOGETHER

The Monkey Mind/dump the c*** exercise

Prompt:

Imagine that you have achieved the success you want, you have arrived at the position/role , etc., that you want and imagine being interviewed by a magazine for an article: they want to know everything about you — your routine, your exercise program, your home decor, the music you listen to, the books you read and ALL about your **amazing look**. E-V-E-R-Y-T-H-I-N-G.

....

....

....

....

....

....

....

....

....

....

....

Hello again! Yesterday we got rid of excess and inappropriate clothing (the raggedy and too small ones) and today we are going to design a small, basic wardrobe that will look attractive and appropriate for all your lifestyle/business activities and aligned with your new brand/personal style.

Action point

Let's start with the "wearing good underwear and something comfy that it is easy to take off and on" thingy again.

Then, let's revisit day 27:

- *The three chosen attributes/words that sum up your brand*
- *Your new mood board with the selection of images aligned and representative of your new chosen brand and all the examples from Jackie Kennedy/Diana, Princess of Wales and the other successful women you admire and how they communicate through their personal style.*

And now, look at your remaining clothes:
  Pile 1 - the "fit just right" clothes hanging neatly in the wardrobe
  Pile 2 - the "too big" clothes piled on a chair
  Pile 3 - the one-size 'too small" clothes remaining.

Are your clothes (Pile 1, 2 & 3) representative of your new persona and your (career/lifestyle) aspirations? If not right now, could they (by mixing them up, adding accessories , etc.)?

Take some time and mix and match, combine your clothes to produce different looks aligned to your mood board.

. . .

Write up/assemble as many outfits as you can to cover both your professional and leisure time, as minimum at least five different outfits. The more you can use single pieces of clothing to make up different looks the better.

....
....
....
....
....
....
....
....
....
....
....
....
....
....
....
....
....
....
....
....
....
....
....
....
....

You may find that you now have a few items of clothing (from one or all piles) that you have not used at all. Put them away neatly.

You can revisit them in a few weeks and, if you cannot find any use within your new personal style, you can then donate them to charity.

. . .

You may have also noticed that you are missing a few key pieces — clothes or accessories: this is your shopping list.

On the other hand, you should also have quite a few options/looks that represent the "New YOU" from one or all piles; the clothes you've used from **Pile 2**, *the too big ones, you can now definitely take to amend/alter so they fit you better as you know you'll need them.*

The clothes you've used from **Pile 3**, *the one size too small ones, you can take out regularly or keep them in a place where you can see them easily — an incentive to lose those last few pounds/dress size.*

To ensure though that your new personal brand/style becomes second nature, you will need to design and organize your closet in a simple manner, with practical use in mind.

There are different ways to arrange clothes and accessories:

- *By category*
- *By color group*
- *By outfit.*

The important thing is to use a system that works for you, is easy to follow and doesn't require too much thinking (especially at the beginning when you are still road-testing your new brand).

. . .

Now select your system and organize your entire wardrobe accordingly (category — color group — outfit).

....
....
....
....
....
....
....
....
....
....
....
....
....
....
....
....
....
....
....

You should now have:

- A freshly clean closet and drawers
- A small (or big depending how many clothes you had to start with) wardrobe that is fully aligned with your new/upgraded personal style/brand that can take you seamlessly from work to leisure with ease.

Great job!

3 things to be thankful for

Think back at the topic covered today — what are the 3 things you are grateful for, despite everything? Remember, if you can't think of any — you are not looking hard enough. Think again.

....
....
....
....
....
....
....
....
....
....
....
....
....
....
....
....
....
....
....
....
....
....
....
....
....

DAY 30: NEXT STEPS

The Monkey Mind/dump the c*** exercise

Prompt:

Future

....
....
....
....
....
....
....
....
....
....
....
....
....
....
....

Launching and promoting your new brand

Now that you've developed your brand, what do you do with it?

Well, now that you have created a personal brand, you need to advertise it. Everyone needs to know about it — it doesn't do any good if it is just in your mind or stays in this workbook.

What you need to do is to communicate what makes you different and helping people frame you in their mind. It is easy: after all they can only evaluate what you show them and it is possible to take control over situations by being consistent and conscious of the messages you send.

And the more you tell people about your new label/brand, the easier it will become.

Two important lessons taken from Marketing 101:

1. Brand consistency is absolute key — same as in advertising, your brand image must remain the same every time the consumer (your boss, prospective boss, investors, family etc.) is exposed to it
2. Brand recall — this essentially measure of how easily people remember what the brand stands for (the three attributes/words). This is crucial to establish the brand.

Consistency is the easier one to achieve:
from now on, everything that you do, wear, say and write about yourself should be consistent with your new/revamped personal style/brand.

. . .

And this means everything that you do, wear, say and write about yourself with your family, friends, your Nan, your dates etc.etc. including a complete review of <u>ALL</u> your social media profiles (yes, that's right): LinkedIn, Instagram, Facebook, Pinterest and any other you might have.

Remember: you are an actor fully immersing yourself in your character, your best self.

Brand recall will be highly dependent on both actively advertising your new brand and the consistency in which you are applying it (after all, you can't say one thing and do another).

Think about a product re-launch: you are about to embark into a massive "New YOU" advertising drive to reach new markets and customers (your new company/position) and upgrade/reposition the views your current customers and markets have of you.

Whether consciously or not, you advertise yourself constantly.

This time it will be a conscious effort, starting with a slow transition with the nearest and dearest, a.k.a. your family and friends. I'm assuming here that you are not likely to be able to "disappear" and not see them for a prolonged period of time. Plus they've known you all their and your life so you'll need to work a bit longer and skillfully to shift their perceptions.

The idea is to project your new/upgraded brand (the three chosen positive attributes together with the associated look) to them in a subtle way.

. . .

The Neuro-Linguistic Programming technique of Mirroring and Matching can be very useful to reinforce and shift your message.

Mirroring is one of the most useful NLP techniques there are, is innate and even chimps use mirroring within their groups.

Pay attention whether people are visual, audial, or kinaesthetic (you do so by listening to their language patterns) and consequently adapt your communication/language style to suit the specific audience and have more impact.

State	Primary sense	Language patterns
Visual	Sight	I see; it looks good
Audial	Hearing	Sounds good; that rings a bell
Kinaesthetic	Feeling	That doesn't feel right; I can't put my finger on it

How?

Start by selecting a few people that have the widest impact amongst your family and friends (the more mouthy and opinionated, once they get it, they will help "spreading the message" and your new brand).

Allow yourself a few weeks to embed the message and make each interaction count: beside wearing your "new clothes", drop hints during casual conversation introducing your three main brand attributes.

. . .

As you interact with them, remember to use "right" language for your audience in line with their primary state and sense (I see, I hear, I feel).

To introduce your new brand in your current workplace/work environment, you have a couple of options:

1. Straight after the weekend spent re-arranging your wardrobe (or a weekend); or
2. A "big reveal" e.g. after an holiday.

If you choose option 1, you can use the same tactics used with your family and friends: pick five people (the ones with the most influence and wider net, must include your boss) and make a conscious effort to reinforce your brand in each and every interaction.

If you choose option 2, "The big reveal", I'd suggest firstly preparing the so-called "30-second commercial", a ready- made pitch to sell your new brand. Make it short, make it snappy and ensure you use the three attributes of your brand in a catchy phrase describing your metamorphosis. This way when people ask you about your new look, you'll have something ready that you have practiced and positions the way you want.

People should be able to remember your brand easily, be able to describe you "the right way" and repeat this accurately to others.

You'll know this is working when:

- People look like they positively recognize your description/attributes when you talk about it
- People start describing you that way to others
- People start inviting you to events, talk to you about projects , etc., aligned with your new brand (after all the purpose of all this is to get you your next coveted position).

Ok then, now it's the time to make some decisions and plan the way forward.

Action point

Look back at the three main attributes/words that describe your "new" brand and the Monkey Mind/dump the c*** media profile of the new you.

Review it, refine it and make sure you re-iterate the three attributes/words throughout the piece.

....
....
....
....
....
....
....
....
....
....
....

Now, crystalize and summarize your media profile into a short and sweet 30-second commercial for the New You.

....
....
....
....
....
....
....
....
....
....
....

Mirror and Match practice = identify five key people amongst your family and friends that you can start to Mirror and Match (be careful not to come across as parroting) and talk about your new brand attributes/showcase your new brand. It would be useful to start with people that have the same language patterns you have (e.g., Visual/Audial/Kinaesthetic) — this will make it much easier. Plan how you will approach the subject/introduce your new brand attributes and schedule over the course of the next few weeks.

....
....
....
....
....
....
....
....
....
....
....
....

Repeat the exercise for people with different language patterns from yours. Plan and schedule.

....
....
....
....
....
....
....
....
....
....
....
....

Mirror and Match practice = identify now the five people at work that you are going to carry out the same practice with. As before, plan how you will approach the subject/introduce your new brand attributes and schedule over the course of the next few weeks.

....
....
....
....
....
....
....
....
....
....
....
....

Irrespectively if you are opting for a "big reveal" or not in your current workplace/work environment, you'll need it anyway for new opportunities outside your work circle. Planning would be good here (hint, hint)....

....
....
....
....
....
....
....
....
....
....
....
....

3 things to be thankful for

Think back at the topic covered today — what are the 3 things you are grateful for, despite everything? Remember, if you can't think of any — you are not looking hard enough. Think again.

....
....
....
....
....
....
....
....
....
....
....
....
....
....
....
....
....
....
....
....
....
....
....
....
....

ONE LAST THING

You have made through the workbook: you should be proud of yourself for keeping up a routine that works towards your development and empowerment.

Now it's when the real work begins, if you quit now, you will miss the best part of your hero journey, the real adventure — when put into practice what you have learned and take action.

I would suggest you continue the journey with the next workbook of course. But whatever you decide, take action and follow through.

And, more than anything, remember these 3 things:

1. Perfection does not exist, Be awesome instead
2. Anything is possible
3. We are all in this together: if we can take care of one another, appreciate each other, we all gain — women inspiring and empowering other women.

And when you start making excuses and blame someone remember:

STOP IT! It is all in your head

AUTHOR'S NOTE

Thank you so much for reading and (hopefully working through) *Look The Part*.

I hope you enjoyed this workbook and it has challenged and perhaps overthrown some of your negative beliefs about yourself. A review would be much appreciated as it helps other readers discover the story. Thanks.

If you sign up for my newsletter you'll be notified of give-aways, new releases and receive personal updates from behind the scenes of my business and books.

Go to www.thepeoplealchemist.com to get started.

Bibliography

I read a lot of books as part of my research. Some of them together with other references include:

Write For Your Life - **Lawrence Block**
The Artist Way - **Julia Cameron**
Tools of Titans - **Tim Ferriss**
Psycho-Cybernetics - **Maxwell Maltz**
Self Mastery Through Conscious Autosuggestion - **Émile Coué**

Printed in Great Britain
by Amazon

83735025R00102